INK AND IMPRESSIONS

An Echo in Parts

Shubhankar Patil

ty to use, or
ency of the

ʒ Platform

Dedication

This collection is for every heart,
that beats to a different rhythm,
and for every soul
that seeks meaning in chaos.

May an echo or two
find its way to you.

Preface

This book is a piece of my heart.

These poems came to me in quiet moments and loud ones - during laughter, and sometimes through tears. These are of unexpectedly days and almost - sleepless nights, when I needed to let something out or hold on to something that still mattered.

Each poem carries a little story, a feeling, a thought I didn't want to lose. Some refused to leave me until they spilled out. Some are deeply personal, while are just observations of the world around me. But all of them carry something meaningful - a beautiful possibility, a confession that frees the soul a little, a moment of happiness too big to be kept inside or a shared experience that we all go through.

I hope as you read, you find something that resonates with you - something familiar, something relatable or even something that makes you see things a little differently.

Thank you for picking this up and letting my words into your world.

your world.

With warmth,

Shubhankar

Acknowledgements

This little book of poems wouldn't exist without a lot of love, patience, and support.

To my family - especially Aai, Baba, my younger brother Swapnil - and my friends: thank you for listening to my rambles, and letting me be my truest self. You've held space for my words long before they made it onto paper.

To the small things—late-night thoughts, passing conversations, quiet walks, and unexpected emotions— thank you for inspiring me when I wasn't even looking.

To my dear friend, Rajkumar Nandrekar, for all of this happened because you thought that I needed a *push* - thank you so much.
To you, *Raji Aaji*...for you are with me always, in the form of the *belief* that you've always had in me. It's the same as *Lord Shiva's trident - it doesn't let me stay down, even if I fall.*

And finally, to you, the reader—thank you for giving these poems your time. It means more than I can say.
With love,
Shubhankar

1. The Final Homecoming

That day morning, I woke up startled
Strange as it was, my mind attempted to thwartle
For the same sinking feeling didn't show up before
With visuals so real, sound effects and more!

I was standing at a shore, letting go of a hand
The figure disappearing in water, my feet rooted to the
sand
But what clear sight revealed, was actually that was
strange
For the figure disappearing and at the shore, were the
same

My life felt good, except this deep sinking feeling
Friends whom I pleased, and future so appealing
The more that dream made sense, the more I realised
This fear of missing out, and feeling deprived

For every possession I thought, that somebody may like
I also had something, that somebody may dislike

Things that I attempt, and chase that I follow
People pleasing is a drug, but a poison hard to swallow

As it dawned to me, the dream reappeared
But the strange feeling and haunt, had disappeared
For what I realised, was fulfilling and empowering to me
Just a living lie I overlooked, my truth that I avoided to
see

*As the figure disappearing and at the shore, were both
me*
Letting go of myself had been sulking, sinking me
For no one to please now, and a chase no more
The waters appear still, and I lay contended at the shore.

2. A Warrior's Shining Armour

When your head soars high, but you're also so low
When your eyes flare anger, but there are tears below
When you're hell motivated, and sharpen your axe
But getting out of the bed too, feels like a task

When your face does smile, but eyes refuse co operation
When your brain analyses everything, but also there's no operation
When you're a skilled swimmer, but also drowning low
When your skills fail but there's land at below

It's okay to learn and cry, when laughing is a task
You ought to be happy, it's all that we ask
This is what suits the warrior, her armour to shine brighter
The world is good then, and every burden is lighter..

3. Only A Memory

My mind is stuck on you and my heart screams like
anything
But all that my surroundings allow is to let out a sigh
I still have your book with rose but now it is withered
Know that my heart has become same as the rose.

Trust seems a familiar word now, something that I
briefed upon only until recently
And now I'm searching for ways, I can be deceived
I was willing to face anything, that came between us
Only now praying that I don't have to face you!

You're long gone, but my hand is still in your direction
Waiting to be clasped by yours, now shaking in pain
Just know that you'll always be a beautiful memory
But alas..that's what. Only a Memory...

4. Whispers To The Trident

As I stand before you, oh *homie divine*

Do you point at you in me, denoting you are mine?

Your footrest counts my echo, as if the shrine expects for me

Though I'm not the only one, he's aware enough to see..

Maybe this signifies a soul tie, as we go hand in hand

Shaking knees - facing life, *your trident makes me stand!*

Maybe it's not just Nandi Maharaj, who conveys everything that I mutter

It's you who stands with decisive hands, with answers to that I suffer!

'Is pain a destiny?' everybody asks, that which makes all banter

Past life karmas - present life decisions? - it has no precise answer!

With my average capacities at reach, this is all I say

He includes all with no differences, eternal peace at his bay...

5. No Floor, No Escape

Hickory Dickery Dock, the clock struck one!
The mouse ain't up the clock, this *isn't* about fun!
For who's up - it's Neil, sensing a presence around
Naked eyes could claim for sure, nothing was to be found!

The guy calmed down saying, maybe it's a lie
To believe this in the morning, I'd rather die!
Saying this he turned around, then facing the mirror,
In sometime he closed his eyes, only to realise the terror!

Wait a minute, he said out loud - If there's no light around..
How is *my reflection visible*, no logic to be found!
I'll access the switch board first, maybe then to the door
But wait what's going on here, THE BED HAS BECOME THE FLOOR!!

As it was of *partial* control, the gestures made it clear
It was a girl bit younger to him, mute but able to hear

The next sight was an interesting one, *flying* BOOKS in the room
Our guy thought it's all over, everything seemed at doom!

Oh sure it did calm down, with pages of books in order..
Maybe it did *reveal* something, asking him to surrender!
As he decided to better negotiate, sensing the business with it..
The soul revealed it meant no harm, there's a *prime culprit!*

A wealthy family mourned the fact, the girl was born mute!
Every facility was to access, a unified sadness acute..
That day was an eventful day, when she fell a bit ill..
The uncle decided to take care of her, while others had task to fulfill

It was by chance to grab some water, the girl moved around..
Startled to know the *extramarital scene,* she'd overheard the sound
The uncle had her *asphyxiated,* jamming the garage door..
The family was shattered by the loss, her body was on the floor

All she wanted was *partial* control, to guide Neil to the
past
The device had captured all that was hidden, it was a
chance - her last!
As Neil agreed to the only chance, to get rid of the
matter
A question lingered still to his mind, that which made
him stutter..

Out of all the countless people, why was it only he?
What was it that others couldn't do, what did she exactly
see?
To this the soul replied, of Neil against the neighbour
Compassion to innocent animals, was a rare sight to
harbour..

But that was not an exact answer, the soul made it clear
There was a particular specific reason, for all the chaos
and tear
*No help out of compassion anymore, a need to be
blackmailed or feared*
Saying this the soul signaled - TO JUSTICE..! - before she
disappeared...

6. A Soul Family

When the paths part ways, and you know it's time
When words fall short, left with expressions and mime
When you get how it is, but you don't want it to be
When it's an obvious plain view, but *your eyes thwart to
see..*

Found a piece of mine, unexpectedly in people around
*Was that conversation expected, to feel like lost and
found?*
Time deepens bond they say, that does hold some ground
*Nothing like an overthinkers relief, because close friends
are around..*

Things did take a turn, both ugly and nice
You found each other in virtue, and caught unexpectedly
in vice
Got to learn from each other, to drop and to imbibe
*It's okay to ask for support, if alone is difficult to
survive..*

Bonds will remain as they are, not everything fades away
Association turns into contact, 'busy' is slogan of the day
You abruptly bump into each other, taking a moment to
reconcile
You are back again to where it was, *a plainland is again
fertile..*

You realise at a moment, that it's okay to drift away
Life is mostly like a swing, a swing is meant to sway
No matter how busy it gets, still it's safe to say
Little worn out maybe, some bonds are meant to stay...

7. A Stained Wing

My eyes had ceased to express, when it hurt the most
Numbness in all my senses, the night had ceased to host
It was all as usual around, with Jasmine of a kind
It all felt just useless as if, peace was rare to find..

"Were you at all undue careless?" - my mind made me
reason
"It's all upto you no matter what" was a line of season by
season
Was left alone to stand by myself, when I raised my
voice
Groping - a medium for quiet suppression, left me with
no choice..

Expectations were always a cage, gender was their base
My wings made me break the barrier, was always a
rebellious case
What feels like a stained wing, despite a powerful flight
Someone close had groped me then, expecting to
suppress my plight.

8. Calories And Confessions

For *every single one* who says, it's just a basic need
May I disagree with all my heart, and a right place to
feed
For I live for few good reasons, and food does top the list
Rasgulla, Biryani and Naan, a major reason to exist..

They speak of two ways to live, like survival and
pleasure
Maybe also a third type like me, *to think of food in
leisure*
Don't consider me for preference concerns, in sweet and
in spicy
So many options make it tricky, *turning my choices
dicey..*

Maybe this all for a limited time, till I'm frail and old
Travel I may or I may not, these are the tales to be told
Sue my appetite if you want, and you are free to judge
With more cuisines than phone contacts, and no
intention to budge...

9. The Kolkata Comeback

Gimmick was it of a score board, with an almost 'all
down' ?
All of the anxious fans wondered, was India to be a
clown?
Was it all ideal at all, with one man firm and tall?
Or was it yet all to be decoded, with team heading a fall?

Nope he was not almighty, neither of a convenient case
A story of precise decision this is, one of *resilience and
faith*
'The Wall' decided to defend it all, with all that he had
An expert to witness of his then condition, was probable
to call him mad..

With a fever of 102, and body full of cramps
A position of 'defender' stamped upon him, not of
convenient champs
On a normal day with all of this, who'll think of giving a
try
Dravid made a decision that day, to be either ride or die..

Both looked like *a pair of Avengers*, the other of VVS by
name
Have you heard of Thor and Loki? - *consider these the
same*
History was to be made that day, with two of gems on
ground
*India was prepared for a reveal, to a pair of lost and
found..*

Wasn't of course easy at all, to pull the test all day
With some pain killers as surviving kit, no chance there
of foul play
*VVS played with a sprained spinal chord, and an firm
resolve to defend*
Australia saw of Resilient Indians, *by a pair with saline
at the end...*

10. Varied Saplings

As I battle with destiny, with not a sound so loud
Does ever anyone looks down to say, *I'm really proud?*
Is it really a question whether, some do have it easy?
Jealousy maybe more common than ever, *a pattern to be
tired and dizzy..*

Why is it always so, that nothing ever is enough?
To be knowing where to stop, maybe that's what is
tough?
Maybe a tryst with destiny, is not a cry alone
What it looks like differs maybe, *varied saplings per seed
sown..*

You may look down upon yourself, maybe it feels let
down
We topple down closest to the reward, left feeling like a
clown
But I think the catch is that (cliche it may sound)
You always begin from experience again, just don't look
around...

11. On Lease

The usual hour passes by, scrolling through my phone,
Lying lazy on the bedside — tired and alone.
The content there just passes by, as I mindlessly scroll
Nothing tends to hold my mind, *as I grapple from the soul...*

Always doubting hidden meanings in what others say —
"You call yourself unique, huh? Pardon, if I may?"
As scratches reveal through surfaces, meanings tend to cease
Overthinking waters self-doubt, while logic is on lease.

Don't you think to be at peace is something that I want?
Just don't say good things to me - to accept it, I can't.
As someone always made believe that simple things are rare,
Do I tend to care too much, while preferred to be unfair?

Guess my choices are a mess, trying to make some sense.
They say you find true peace within - is it of any

essence?
While my mind boggles illusions, *with easy escape routes*
A tendency down some slippery slope, *where endings grow as shoots...*

12. Roaring And Resilient

Your veins carry boiling blood and the soul seeks hope,
Climbing the mountain barefoot, with no sign of a rope,
When your body grows frail, maybe, do let out a sigh —
Being an Indian, may I remind, dare *never say die!*

Soil of this holy land has an imprint on your soul —
Sikh, Gorkha, Maratha, and Dogra — different flavours of
a bowl.
Never have a count to know how many you dare;
Your cause is a worthy one — you don't have to care.

Dizzy, confused and terrified — one day you may grog
Always a struggle it has been, *to not be an underdog.*
Soul may wither from different wounds, maybe making
you soar —
Remember, you're soul of a lion, always bound to roar!

A river may turn into a stream, but it'll never dry.
Roaring and resilient is my blood — of no use it is to try.

Go out there and you may check, going door to door —
Whether a cub or a lion, it's always bound to roar!!

13. Pocket - Sized Peace

Alas, it marked the weekend's arrival—finally, it was time.
An entire room of tangled mess, and the task was mine.
Mess as it truly was, but what more could it be?
Stamps of a life till then were all that I could see.

Beyblade coronated all of it—nothing short of an obsession.
A single place for an entire day was mostly a choice for position!
It would just there roll along, spinning around the ring,
Reminding me just maybe, that *happiness is a simple thing.*

If I want to list it all, a full day isn't enough.
To describe here as all of it, honestly, would be a bluff.
But I can point out to you of what meant to me—
A few items for a list, but a happy face to see!

As I look back all along, a lot of it has changed—

Beyblade, to Yoyo, to books and phone—much more
things have ranged.
But if I were at all to ask, what it was truly—
That which makes you happy, at peace, to be alive
fully?

No *'Eureka..!'* always it is—*no need for it to be.*
Brick by brick of my childhood can compel you to see:
It wasn't much, but always enough—have you wondered
why?
The answers you seek are mostly simple; just do dare to
try!

14. Holding A Paw

As I strive along the path, of a journey called life
Pretty faces pretend to smile, like butter along the knife
Never claimed to know it all, I know that it's not me,
A real life with less of drama is what you fail to see.

With fake smiles and formal hugs - you pretend to be friendly,
Visible tears when I'm sad is ignored by convenience - daily.
Funny it is for you to think, your validation it is I need
Your inner void is visible enough as drama is your feed.

Couldn't understand of my eyes, as I soaked in tears
Still a way my friend had found, wise beyond his years
Stroking a paw through my head, a relief I tend to feel
Will face it all and rise in pain, *his presence will make me heal*!

15. Moonlight Minds

As I look down from the window, with darkness around,
The silent colony blinks at me, devoid of any sound.
As I look at the street lamps that emit a bit of light,
this silence is of much more peace than hours of sleep at
night.

Unusually different from the usual crowd, early ones call
you "owl,"
Puffy eyes - not a lofty price, although *attracting a scowl.*
You may mark your end of the day with the usual setting
sun -
We, the people of gentle moon - which can count on fun.

As I stare at the midnight sky, admiring the pleasant
moon,
My mind may feast on creative take, with gentle breeze
as spoon.
You may seem to wonder why these people stay awake—
Listen to the silence such hours have; peace all yours to
take.

As I say, on a conclusive end, this is the magic of night:
Escaping the buzz of that day, your mind may take a
flight.
As you fall in love with darkness that *covers the magic
around—*
It's here, in such dark and quiet, *a piece of you to be
found.*

16. As a Man

Just put on a happy face; I see no other way
To define myself as a *man*—this is the way to say.
As the usual schedule moves along, I mumble to myself:
Always a demand on the go, another jar on the shelf.

To my plethora of emotions, which outlet do I find?
A way to control my all my angst *is an achievement of a
kind.*
Realisation hitting hard—as the setting sun I see—
Exactly what is allowed to feel? Just explain it to me.

Another day is marked to end as I grab the pillow,
How my day has really been, *no one bothers to know.*
Flipping on either side of bed, a question I seem to see:
Exactly what am I supposed to feel? Just explain it to me.

17. A Curious Case

As I chill with *Enid Blyton*, my childhood prodigy,
A question at the back of my mind starts pestering me:
What was it that made me curious - why did I opt to
read?
What made me differ from usual kids—what was sown as
a seed?

Of mine was a curious case—neither self-help nor
history;
The genre that I feasted on was *crime, thriller, and
mystery!*
Unusual (or disappointing, is it?) to enjoy what I did,
Perhaps the reason for elders to frown—I was only a kid.

But honestly, what a thrill it was to know of *Sherlock
Holmes!*
Through the famous *Bakers Street*, my mind still
sometimes roams.
Through history, fiction, and other streams, I later
became a fan,

*But this is where the seed was sown - this is where all
began!*

18. Behind The Quiet

Pleasant it is to be with me, if you see for as I am;
Erupting thoughts like water in my mind — call it an entire dam.
Just don't know what exactly to say when you approach me;
My face does speak with loss of words, if you'll closely see.

Not really it is that I'm rude — just a bit socially shy;
Open talk with you in my mind, as you interact by.
If, by chance, you stop to speak, it'll be so much delight;
Open up to the fun you'll see, as my thoughts take flight.

Maybe *I'll disappear for a while, as a recharge to stay alive;*
Understand that's how I function — maybe just socially naive.
A whole spectrum is open to show, once it's comfy with you;

Maybe we'll switch roles for you to listen — even that's possible too!

19. The Battle With Dawn

As the dawn of a new day comes, the alarm buzzes
again,
Getting up is not an issue; early morning is of pain.
They instruct me to get early to bed, but I can't even
blink;
Goodness knows how you doze off early, *with so much
of time to think.*

That's not even half of the story — the monster is yet to
come:
*Procrastination, as the noble ones call, yet he's familiar
to some.*
You can't even blame him as he strikes — how comfy he
is to be,
*Till he becomes quite close to you; it's always hard to
see.*

All I want to imply is that it's not that I complain;
To live rightly, you've to take the right amount of strain.
As I come to terms with the way which I deep down

know,
A bit of understanding would do — for me, it's a hard pill
to swallow.

20. A Scoop Of Delight

The child in me will never die, as long as this exists;
My bank account will carry a load, trailing to these visits.
Different flavours of tasty delight that these people display —
Pista, Coffee, Chocolate, and more too awestruck to say.

My taste may change, of considerable times, into adulthood through;
I'll grab a different flavour than before, maybe too good to be true.
A peculiar kid, that I am, I do like a brand;
I may go without having one, if I can't withstand.

One of the ways of consoling me could be a flavour on-demand,
Negotiating on upper hand, maybe, is what I can command.
I may look back on those flavours once I turn up old,

And then be a child for a few flavours again, with a story to be told.

21. Of Laughter, Tears And Charlie

A peculiar guy lights up the screen as I stare in awe.
He does something, *and you don't laugh — it's a breach of the law.*
You'll never call him someone smart, nor does he look handsome,
But when he carries the screen with him, it'll be awesome.

Always someone you do stop by — someone to be laughed at —
Worn-out coat, and patched-up shirt, and maybe a hole in the hat.
His peculiar moustache will make you giggle; he calls himself Charlie,
A tear or two at the corner of an eye as you watch him being silly.

Always a conflict: to be human or to find some work.
Honest he is, and he does try, only to be called a jerk.

Then he walks in his peculiar style, unknowingly telling
a tale,
*Where empty stomach is an everyday scene and morale
is up for sale.*

The ending will leave you mostly in splits as he makes
you think.
Most of the time, he loses something, only to be saved at
the brink.
He keeps you at the edge of your seat when he hatches a
plan.
*If, after a movie, you search for the next, welcome to the
clan.*

22. Beyond The Filters

As I wander along the path of drama and cold war,
It makes me wonder most of the time what makes them
go this far.
As they post unlimited pics of *babe and pookie,*
It's a trade along the path, *too steep and tricky.*

So easy it is, no matter what, to just do what you want.
How strange it is to pretend to do all that you possibly
can't.
Filter - not a feature anymore of online interface;
It's become a part of people's lives, to show them on their
face.

And then the same ones question me why I prefer a few.
Preferable it is to be intact and have some quality too.
No matter how many happy pics your social media
shows;
The slightest change your life goes through, each one of
them knows.

Not having a call for months along is a frequent way to
be,
With our lives at constant slog - for several months no
see.
If at all a call happens though - in the middle of a phase,
To know that they'll have my back is a matter of solace.

23. Through My Eyes

The closer I try to have a look, the more distant it seems;
For sure some sort of mystery it is, like a few of my dreams.
The more I try to feel the same, the more alien it goes;
Seems like it's a lonely birth with neither friends nor foes.

For a while, please let me know how all of this exactly works —
To have a proper family then, please let me know the perks:
When you have a pair of two who care for you too much,
And a space to confide in, no restrictions as such.

Blessed by fortune, if you are, you'll find a tribe too;
As you grow, it gets difficult — and they will see you through.
And if you want to still complain, just have a look at me;
Maybe you'll get convinced - it's still not lonely to be.

24. Lost In The Lush

Let me lie in this still and quiet.
You may wonder a bit, till I get out of the sight.
To not move and soak everything around—
May smell the bushy air and kiss a bit of the ground.

It may make no sense at all, as I may stare at blank.
My mind may think of memories long before they sank—
And no thought at large at all, or it may feel that way;
No voice to ring at my ears, nothing for me to say.

As I feel the lushness around and the aroma I smell,
All the green of several years, with a heap of stories to
tell.
I fear to probably lose my track, or shift here forever—
Or you may try to locate me, as I engage in this
endeavour.

25. Codename: Nobody

Did you wonder who was I
when you were just passing by?
I may smirk, just in my mind,
as I'm one of a kind.

Concerned, of course, I'll be,
if you care to notice me.
Don't ever bother to ask my name,
for every time, *it'll not be the same.*

Don't wreck your mind on tracking us;
you'll never be able to figure it out.
You'll never know *the lengths we scale*
to make the entire threat pass out.

To introduce us, they call us squad;
we have no legit, particular face.
Consider us to be *anonymous*
till the threats resurface!

26. Of Seven Minutes

As I close my eyes finally, just let me pass through.
I do die with a happy heart, by living full and true.
Maybe you'll have a turn, as my seven minutes begin,
Let me have a glimpse at ones with me through thick
and thin.

A clean slate—not entirely it is—that maybe I've had.
Some of my chapters appear *alien*; some will make you
sad.
Some will make you think about what you're going
through,
*Some may make you decide better at what you want to
do.*

Some may shriek you, probably, and scared to open the
book.
*I do confess of some mistakes, some dead ends where I
shook.*
At some pages, I made amends, and at some, I've tried.
I polished all my chapters well to give you a jolly ride.

Maybe this is the end of what the seven minutes had
been.
They say no one can pretend here— of all is heard and
seen.
So, you see that at my last, I cannot prefer to lie:
*What is better than having you all at the exact time I
die?*

27. I'll Say Irfan

Of no grand stature or of fame,
He worked so hard to carry a name—
A name that every stage may know,
To which all beginners take a bow.

They speak so widely of his eyes,
A story his expressions could suffice.
Don't bother to look for flashy fame,
But *a set of eyes* that carry a name.

Whether it's *Karwaan or Life of Pi,*
An expression is enough to make you cry.
At one end some philosophy - for you to know;
At other, a gut - wrenching emotion to show.

They tend to speak about the human he was—
He'd speak his mind, and time would take a pause.
A synonym for pride in Hindi is Shaan;
You'll mention of eyes, and I'll say Irfan.

28. Through My Desk

Not an exact answer when you ask me why;
May not make sense, but let me try.
I began to write as a channel for me,
I articulate less but set myself free.

My desk did seem like an all-time mess—
Of some inscribed waste, and I couldn't care less.
That's generally how it goes for maybe those who write:
A jumble through the words till clarity shines bright.

At the most crucial moments, *you may be all alone,*
Overwhelming emotion and pain through each bone.
At exact such moments,a paper lies by;
Pain fuels the paragraphs, and you let out a sigh.

It's an unexpected route to lead through inner pile
To discover a puzzle or find a hidden vile
Some may have an influence, as the paper you express
on —
Who knows, you may inspire, and a writer will be born!

29. A Monsoon Moment

Monsoon had already appeared by then; I can remember
still.
Year-end was sometime before, the wind was turning
chill.
I'd almost bumped into her; it was a unique feel,
*A face that beauty bowed down to, every charm would
kneel.*

All of it rolled out to be like a slow-motion scene;
Her presence had all appeared like, an influence so keen.
Just as I'd thought to move, she gleamed a pretty smile.
Afraid to make her conscious, *I stumbled upon a tile.*

Lost in her world, she was, had everything else on hold.
*Her hair had shone of glimmering tinge, with eyes of
tales untold.*
Maybe she'll appear again; that's all to hope for now.
She'll stumble upon a tile someday, but don't know when
and how.

30. The Pause

I call myself in love - but an idiot, am I?
With the *potential of a banyan, am I being bonsai?*
I scroll through reels, in galleries, I breathe,
Only to miss your grin - those smiling teeth.

I lose myself in hopes - or hopeless, should I say?
You water a plant so much, *only for it to decay.*
I force myself to sleep, then wake up seeking cause..
What has become of me? My life has hit a pause.

I hope one day we cross paths - and that you truly stop,
Consider me, just once, to feel over the top.
I listen to you patiently - with all your 'if' and 'why',
Only to disagree with it all..and wave a satisfied bye.

31. On a Count of Three

As I stroll along this path and strain a bit to see,
Can't believe you came along and chose to be with me.
It can feel weirdly different at times of days and nights,
Streets make you shiver with cold while sometimes you
take flights

Maybe you'll scowl at me - too abrupt a tale
Elegance may not lunge around and logic fails to sail.
Still I see you flip the page and pause along with me,
Till we turn to a different lane on a count of three.

Every road does lead somewhere, and it goes on and on,
Sometimes you get to be the king, at times you're a
pawn.
*But every journey does come to an end, as we may mark
today,*
We will surely meet again - for now, that's all I say.